BOLD UNIQUE JEWELRY

It's easy to make a fearless fashion statement! Simply combine eccentric beads, chains, and other elements that reflect your personal style.

LEISURE ARTS, INC. • Maumelle, Arkansas

SHOPPING LIST

- ☐ 3 20mm faceted clear beads
- ☐ 6 15mm gunmetal beads
- ☐ 5 15mm faceted antique silver beads
- ☐ 4 15mm faceted clear beads
- ☐ 10 10mm grey pearl beads
- ☐ 8 10mm faceted black beads
- ☐ 15 3mm black seed beads
- ☐ 3 3mm silver daisy spacer beads
- ☐ 38" length of heavy gunmetal chain
- ☐ gunmetal lobster clasp
- ☐ 6 5mm gunmetal jump rings
- ☐ 2 7mm gunmetal jump rings
- ☐ 18 black eye pins
- ☐ 18 black head pins
- ☐ chain-nose pliers (2 pair)
- ☐ round-nose pliers
- ☐ wire cutters

METALLIC BAUBLE NECKLACE

*Be sure to read the **General Instructions** on pages 30-32 before making your project.*

Necklace Finished Length: *about 17", excluding bead dangles*

To make the Necklace:

1. From the chain cut:
   - one 16" length
   - one 7 1/2" length
   - one 6 1/2" length
   - one 6" length

2. Use a 7mm jump ring to join the clasp to one end of the 16" chain length. Join the remaining 7mm jump ring to the opposite chain end. Matching the centers, use 5mm jump rings to connect the ends of the 7 1/2" chain length to the 16" chain length.

3. Matching the centers, use 5mm jump rings to join the ends of the 6 1/2" chain length to the 7 1/2" chain length. Repeat to join the 6" chain length to the 6 1/2" chain length.

4. Thread a daisy spacer bead and a 20mm clear bead on a head pin. Make a wrapped loop attaching the head pin to the center of the 16" chain length. Repeat to add the remaining 20mm clear beads to the 16" chain, spacing them about 2" on either side of the center bead dangle.

5. Thread a black seed bead and a gunmetal bead on a head pin. Make a wrapped looped attaching the head pin to the 16" chain length where desired. Repeat to add the remaining gunmetal beads, antique silver beads, and 15mm clear beads, spacing the bead dangles as desired along all 4 chain lengths.

6. Thread a grey pearl bead on an eye pin. Make a wrapped loop, attaching the eye pin to the 16" chain length. Repeat to add the remaining grey pearl beads and black beads, spacing the bead dangles as desired along all 4 chain lengths.

SHOPPING LIST

- ☐ 12 20mm x 25mm fuchsia acrylic oval beads
- ☐ 4 15mm faceted antique silver beads
- ☐ 7 $^{3}/_{4}$" diameter unfinished wood beads
- ☐ 16 4mm silver ball beads
- ☐ 12" length of large link silver chain
- ☐ 4 4mm silver jump rings
- ☐ 4 silver crimp beads
- ☐ 4 silver crimp covers
- ☐ 2 hole/loop silver clasp
- ☐ 49-strand/.018" bead stringing wire
- ☐ aqua acrylic paint and small paintbrush
- ☐ matte finish clear acrylic spray sealer
- ☐ crimp tool
- ☐ chain-nose pliers (2 pair)
- ☐ round-nose pliers
- ☐ wire cutters

DOUBLE STRAND NECKLACE

*Be sure to read the **General Instructions** on pages 30-32 before making your project.*

Necklace Finished Length: *about 16$^{1}/_{2}$"*

To make the Necklace:

1. Allowing to dry between coats, paint the wood beads with 2 coats of aqua paint. Allowing to dry between coats, apply 2-3 coats of sealer to the painted beads.

2. Cut the chain into two 2" lengths and two 2$^{3}/_{4}$" lengths.

3. Use a crimp bead to attach a 14" beading wire length to one end of one 2" chain length. Thread the following beads on the beading wire:
   - silver ball bead, fuchsia bead; repeat a total of 3 times
   - silver ball bead, silver faceted bead
   - 3 aqua painted beads
   - silver faceted bead, silver ball bead
   - fuchsia bead, silver ball bead; repeat a total of 3 times

   Use a crimp bead to attach the beaded strand to one end of the remaining 2" chain length. Cover each crimp bead with a crimp cover.

4. Repeat Step 3 and use a 16" beading wire length, along with the remaining crimp beads, 2$^{3}/_{4}$" chain lengths, beads (use 4 aqua painted beads rather than 3), and crimp bead covers.

5. Use jump rings to attach the strands to the holes/loops of the clasp pieces.

SHOPPING LIST

- ☐ 9 assorted mechanical gears, sprockets, tags, game spinners with pronged fasteners, and a watch face (We used products from Prima Marketing, Inc. and Tim Holtz® Idea-ology scrapbooking product lines.)
- ☐ 4mm antique brass ball bead
- ☐ 4mm antique copper ball bead
- ☐ 14" length of antique gold chain
- ☐ 10-15 7mm antique brass jump rings
- ☐ 5-7 5mm antique brass jump rings
- ☐ 1 5/8" long antique silver key charm
- ☐ antique brass lobster clasp
- ☐ E6000® Industrial Strength Adhesive
- ☐ 1.5mm metal hole punch
- ☐ chain-nose pliers (2 pair)
- ☐ wire cutters

GEARS NECKLACE

*Be sure to read the **General Instructions** on pages 30-32 before making your project.*

***Necklace Finished Length:** about 19", without extension chain*

To make the Necklace:

1. Arrange the assorted gears, sprockets, tags, and watch face in a slightly curved arrangement. Use the larger jump rings to join the pieces through any opening. Use the metal hole punch to make additional holes as needed. Use the smaller jump rings to tightly connect pieces as desired.

2. Use the pronged fastener to attach game spinners to a few of the pieces. Adhere the ball beads to the center of two gears/sprockets. Adhere any additional gears/sprockets to the arrangement as desired.

3. Cut two 5 1/2" chain lengths and a 2" chain length. Use a large jump ring to attach one 5 1/2" chain length to one side of the gear arrangement. Use a small jump ring to attach the clasp to the free chain end.

4. Use a large jump ring to attach the remaining 5 1/2" chain length to the opposite side of the gear arrangement. For the extender chain, use a large jump ring to attach the 2" chain length to the free chain end. Use a small jump ring to attach the key charm to the free end of the 2" chain length.

ARTFUL
1375

SHOPPING LIST

- ☐ 2 20mm x 30mm faceted bronze beads
- ☐ 2 8mm bronze pearl beads
- ☐ 2 8mm rhinestone rondelle beads
- ☐ 17" length of antique copper small link chain
- ☐ 2 gold eye pins
- ☐ 2 antique gold ear wires
- ☐ chain-nose pliers (2 pair)
- ☐ round-nose pliers
- ☐ wire cutters

CHAIN TASSEL EARRINGS

Be sure to read the ***General Instructions*** *on pages 30-32 before making your project.*

To make each Earring:

1. Make a bead connector with a pearl bead, a rondelle bead, a faceted bead, and an eye pin.

2. Cut four 2" chain lengths; trim two of the chain lengths slightly shorter. Attach the chain lengths to the bead connector at the pearl bead end. Attach the ear wire to the remaining end of the bead connector.

SHOPPING LIST

- ☐ unfinished wood bangle bracelet
- ☐ acrylic paint (black and white)
- ☐ small paintbrush
- ☐ 5/8" diameter circle sponge dauber
- ☐ matte finish clear acrylic spray sealer
- ☐ 7mm black acrylic gemstones
- ☐ E6000® Industrial Strength Adhesive

BANGLE BRACELET

*Be sure to read the **General Instructions** on pages 30-32 before making your project.*

To make the Bracelet:

1. Allowing to dry between coats, spray the bracelet with 1-2 coats of spray sealer. Allowing to dry between coats, paint the bracelet with 2 coats of black paint. Allowing to dry between coats, apply 2-3 coats of sealer to the painted bracelet.

2. Use the circle dauber to paint white dots randomly on the bangle, allowing some dots to go off the edges and applying 2-3 coats of paint (allow to dry between coats). Allowing to dry between coats, apply 2-3 coats of sealer.

3. Adhere the gemstones to the full circles on the bracelet. Allow to dry completely.

CHUNKY WOOD NECKLACE

SHOPPING LIST

- ☐ 15 20mm x 28mm brown wood-look rectangular beads
- ☐ 24 6mm x 12mm natural color wood rondelle beads
- ☐ 41 8mm cream beads
- ☐ 164 3mm bronze cube beads
- ☐ 98 3mm x 5mm black rondelle beads
- ☐ 24 6mm antique brass ball beads
- ☐ 56 4mm antique brass ball beads
- ☐ 2 copper cones
- ☐ 8 crimp beads
- ☐ antique brass toggle clasp
- ☐ 2 4mm antique brass jump rings
- ☐ 49-strand/.018" bead stringing wire
- ☐ 18-gauge copper wire
- ☐ crimp tool
- ☐ chain-nose pliers (2 pair)
- ☐ round-nose pliers
- ☐ wire cutters

*Be sure to read the **General Instructions** on pages 30-32 before making your project.*

***Necklace Finished Length:** about 21"*

To make the Necklace:

1. Cut two 6" lengths of 18-gauge wire. Using the round-nose pliers, create a wrapped loop on one end of one wire length. Tighten the wraps with the chain-nose pliers. Repeat with the remaining wire length.

2. Use a crimp bead to attach a 26" stringing wire length to one wire loop ***(Fig. 1)***.

Fig. 1

3. Thread beads on the stringing wire as follows:
   - 7 4mm ball beads, 3 6mm ball beads
   - brown rectangular bead, cube bead; 14 times total
   - brown rectangular bead
   - 3 6mm ball beads, 7 4mm ball beads

   Use a crimp bead to attach the stringing wire to the remaining wire loop.

4. Attach a 26" stringing wire length to a wire loop. Thread beads on the stringing wire as follows:
   - 7 4mm ball beads, 3 6mm ball beads
   - 137 cube beads
   - 3 6mm ball beads, 7 4mm ball beads

   Use a crimp bead to attach the stringing wire to the remaining wire loop.

Continued on page 12.

5. Attach a 26" stringing wire length to a wire loop. Thread beads on the stringing wire as follows:
   - 7 4mm ball beads, 3 6mm ball beads
   - 3 cream beads, 3 wood rondelle beads
   - 5 cream beads, 3 wood rondelle beads; 7 times total
   - 3 cream beads, 3 6mm ball beads, 7 4mm ball beads

   Use a crimp bead to attach the stringing wire to the remaining wire loop.

6. Attach a 26" stringing wire length to a wire loop. Thread beads on the stringing wire as follows:
   - 7 4mm ball beads, 3 6mm ball beads
   - 6 black rondelle beads
   - cube bead, 7 black rondelle beads; 12 times total
   - cube bead, 6 black rondelle beads
   - 3 6mm ball beads, 7 4mm ball beads

   Use a crimp bead to attach the stringing wire to the remaining wire loop.

7. Thread one wire loop through a cone and gently pull until the beaded strands are seated nicely at the cone opening. Make a wrapped loop.

8. Use a jump ring to attach a clasp piece to the wrapped loop.

9. Repeat Steps 7 and 8 with the bead strands, remaining cone, jump ring, and clasp piece.

STATEMENT NECKLACE

Instructions on pages 14-15.

STATEMENT NECKLACE

SHOPPING LIST

- ☐ polymer clay (aqua, fuchsia, lavender)
- ☐ 10 5mm gold jump rings
- ☐ 2 5¹/₂" lengths of gold chain
- ☐ 13 1" gold eye pins
- ☐ gold lobster clasp
- ☐ E6000® Industrial Strength Adhesive
- ☐ deck of playing cards
- ☐ craft knife
- ☐ rolling pin and small baking sheet (dedicated to working with clay; do not use with food)
- ☐ baby wipes
- ☐ wax paper
- ☐ tracing paper
- ☐ chain-nose pliers (2 pair)

*Be sure to read the **General Instructions** on pages 30-32 before making your project.*

***Necklace Finished Length:** about 17¹/₂"*

To make the Necklace:

1. Trace the patterns, below right, onto tracing paper; cut out.

2. Pinch off about half of the lavender clay. Knead and roll the clay in your hand to soften and condition it; roll it into a ball. Lay out two stacks of 18 playing cards each, about 3" apart, on a wax paper covered work surface. Slightly flatten the ball and place it between the card stacks. Using the rolling pin to roll out the clay to the height of the card stacks.

3. Place Pattern A on the clay. Carefully cut out the shape with the craft knife. Using your fingers, smooth the sides and top edges to give the clay a more rounded shape. Set the clay shape aside.

4. Repeat Steps 2 and 3 with the fuchsia and aqua clay, using Patterns B and C to cut aqua shapes and Patterns D and E to cut fuchsia shapes. Be sure to clean the roller and your work surface with a baby wipe between clay colors.

5. Referring to the dots on the patterns, insert eye pins into each clay shape about halfway up the sides so that only the loop of the eye pin is showing ***(Photo 1)***. Follow the manufacturer's instructions to bake the clay shapes.

Photo 1

6. Once the clay shapes have cooled, gently remove each eye pin, dip the pin in adhesive, and reinsert into the clay shape. Allow to dry.

7. Referring to the photo, use jump rings to join the clay shapes together.

8. Use a jump ring to join a chain length to each free eye pin. Attach a jump ring to one chain end. Use the remaining jump ring to attach the clasp to the remaining chain end.

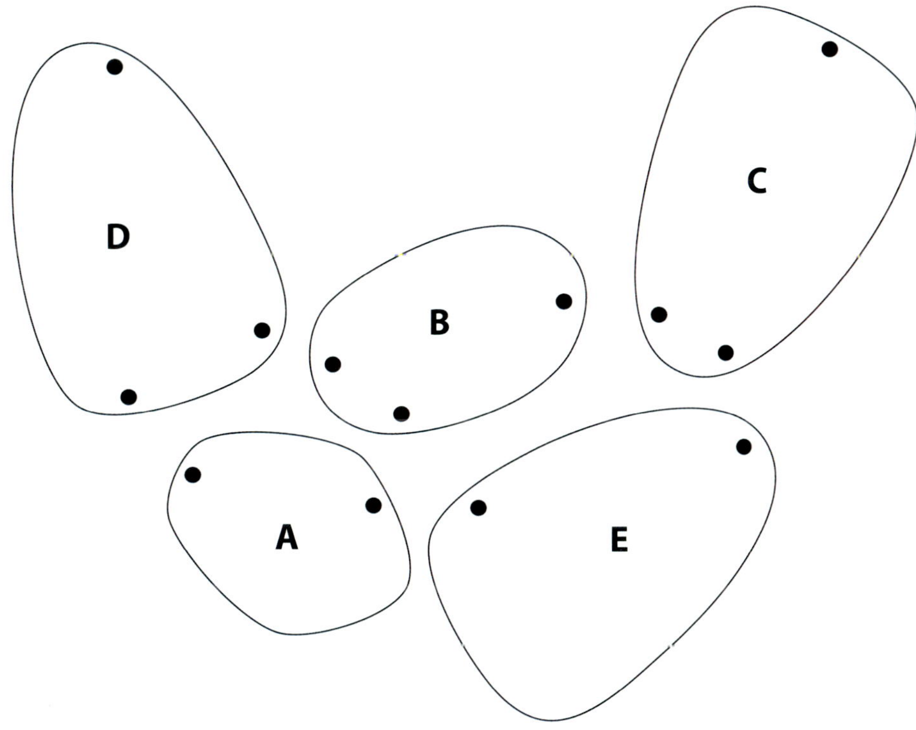

SHOPPING LIST

- ☐ 3 33mm matte black spikes, each with a hanging loop
- ☐ 14 4mm silver ball beads
- ☐ 3 silver eye pins
- ☐ 4 4mm silver jump rings
- ☐ 5mm silver jump ring
- ☐ 2 8" lengths of silver chain
- ☐ silver lobster clasp
- ☐ chain-nose pliers (2 pair)
- ☐ round-nose pliers
- ☐ wire cutters

BLACK SPIKE NECKLACE

*Be sure to read the **General Instructions** on pages 30-32 before making your project.*

***Necklace Finished Length:** about 16 1/2", excluding spikes*

To make the Necklace:

1. Alternating beads and spikes, thread 4 silver ball beads and the black spikes on an eye pin. Make a loop near the end of the eye pin.

2. Thread 5 silver ball beads on an eye pin. Make a loop near the end of the eye pin. Repeat to make a total of 2 beaded eye pins.

3. Attach the beaded/spiked eye pin to one end of each chain length. Lay the chain on a flat work surface and align the links so they are parallel to each other. Attach a beaded eye pin to the chain about 3/8" above the beaded/spiked eye pin. Repeat to attach the remaining beaded eye pin to the chain, placing it about 3/8" above the previous beaded eye pin.

4. Cut the chain links right above the last beaded eye pin. Use a 4mm jump ring to reattach each chain end to the last beaded eye pin. This will keep the beads and chain from twisting.

5. Use a 4mm jump ring to attach the 5mm jump ring to one chain end. Use the remaining 4mm jump ring to attach the clasp to the remaining chain end.

SHOPPING LIST

- ☐ 6 21mm x 37mm lime acrylic teardrop beads
- ☐ 5 18mm x 25mm aqua acrylic teardrop beads
- ☐ 4 12mm x 18mm black acrylic teardrop beads
- ☐ 26 8mm antique gold ball beads
- ☐ 17 8mm gold jump rings
- ☐ 2 4mm gold jump rings
- ☐ 4 gold crimp beads
- ☐ 2 gold fold-over cord ends
- ☐ 49-strand/.018" bead stringing wire
- ☐ 20 1/2" length of 5/8" wide black satin ribbon
- ☐ craft glue
- ☐ crimp tool
- ☐ chain-nose pliers (2 pair)

TEARDROP NECKLACE

Be sure to read the ***General Instructions*** *on pages 30-32 before making your project.*

Necklace Finished Length: *about 24", excluding bead drops*

To make the Necklace:

1. Lay one ribbon end in one fold-over cord end, apply a drop of glue, and use the chain-nose pliers to fold the tabs over the ribbon end ***(Fig. 1)***. Repeat with the opposite end of the ribbon.

Fig. 1

2. Use a 4mm jump ring to connect an 8mm jump ring to each fold-over cord end.

3. Attach an 8mm jump ring to each lime, aqua, and black teardrop bead.

4. Use a crimp bead to attach an 8" stringing wire length to one 8mm jump ring on one ribbon end. Thread 2 antique gold beads and a lime teardrop bead on the wire; repeat for a total of 14 antique gold beads and 6 lime teardrop beads. Use a crimp bead to attach the wire to the 8mm jump ring on the remaining ribbon end.

5. Use a crimp bead to attach an 8" stringing wire length to one 8mm jump ring on one ribbon end. Thread 2 antique gold beads on the wire. Thread an aqua teardrop bead, an antique gold bead, and a black teardrop bead on the wire; repeat for a total of 10 antique gold beads, 5 aqua teardrop beads, and 4 black teardrop beads. Thread on the 2 remaining antique gold beads. Use a crimp bead to attach the wire to the 8mm jump ring on the remaining ribbon end.

SHOPPING LIST

- ☐ 2 12mm x 18mm aqua acrylic teardrop beads
- ☐ 2 gold large chain links
- ☐ 2 8mm gold jump rings
- ☐ 2 gold ear wires
- ☐ chain-nose pliers (2 pair)

TEARDROP EARRINGS

*Be sure to read the **General Instructions** on pages 30-32 before making your project.*

To make each Earring:

1. Use a jump ring to attach an aqua bead to a gold chain link.

2. Attach the chain link to an ear wire.

SHOPPING LIST

- ☐ 61 8mm ecru pearl beads
- ☐ 2 6mm gold ball beads
- ☐ 2 4mm gold ball beads
- ☐ $18^1/_2$" length of large link gold chain
- ☐ 38" length of antique brass chain
- ☐ 13" length of 2mm rhinestone/ gold strand with 2 rhinestone chain ends
- ☐ gold two-hole slider clasp
- ☐ 2 8mm gold jump rings
- ☐ 10 4mm gold jump rings
- ☐ 2 gold crimp beads
- ☐ 49-strand/.018" bead stringing wire
- ☐ crimp tool
- ☐ chain-nose pliers (2 pair)
- ☐ wire cutters

CHAIN & PEARLS NECKLACE

*Be sure to read the **General Instructions** on pages 30-32 before making your project.*

***Necklace Finished Length:** about 18"*

To make the Necklace:

1. Use a crimp bead to attach a 24" stringing wire length to a 4mm jump ring. Thread a 4mm gold bead, a 6mm gold bead, the ecru pearl beads, the remaining 6mm gold bead, and the remaining 4mm gold bead on the wire. Use a crimp bead to attach the beaded strand to a 4mm jump ring. Use the jump rings to attach the beaded strand to one hole on each clasp end.

2. Attach an 8mm jump ring, then a 4mm jump ring to each end of the large link gold chain. Use the 4mm jump rings to attach the chain to the remaining hole on each clasp end.

3. Cut a $19^1/_2$" length and a $17^1/_2$" length from the antique brass chain; set the longer length aside for now. Use 4mm jump rings to attach the $17^1/_2$" length to the same clasp holes as the pearl beaded strand.

4. Attach a rhinestone chain end to each end of the rhinestone chain ***(Fig. 1)***. Center and attach the rhinestone chain to the $19^1/_2$" antique brass chain length with 4mm jump rings. Use 4mm jump rings to attach the antique brass chain to the same clasp holes as the gold chain length.

Fig. 1

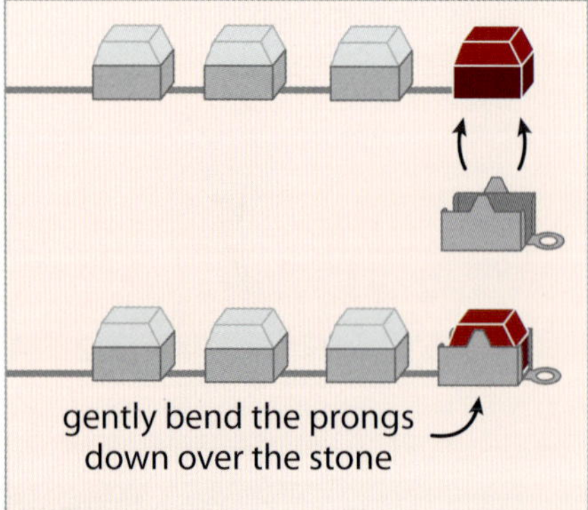

SHOPPING LIST

- ☐ 2 33mm gold spikes, each with a hanging loop
- ☐ 2 8mm gold/rhinestone beads
- ☐ 2 14mm gold/rhinestone connectors
- ☐ 2 gold eye pins
- ☐ 2 4mm gold jump rings
- ☐ 2 gold ear wires
- ☐ chain-nose pliers (2 pair)
- ☐ round-nose pliers
- ☐ wire cutters

GOLD SPIKE EARRINGS

Be sure to read the ***General Instructions*** *on pages 30-32 before making your project.*

To make each Earring:

1. Use an eye pin to make a gold/rhinestone bead connector.
2. Join a spike to the gold/rhinestone bead connector. Join the 14mm connector to the bead connector.
3. Use a jump ring to join the 14mm connector to an ear wire.

STAMPED PENDANT NECKLACE & EARRINGS

Instructions on pages 24-29.

STAMPED PENDANT NECKLACE

SHOPPING LIST

- ☐ 8 10mm teal beads
- ☐ 4 10mm faceted clear beads
- ☐ 8mm faceted clear bead
- ☐ 14 3mm x 5mm lime green rondelle beads
- ☐ 32 5mm x 8mm wooden aqua rondelle beads
- ☐ 8 8mm rhinestone rondelle beads
- ☐ 4-ply brown wax linen cord
- ☐ 12" length of aqua suede lacing
- ☐ 2 silver fold-over cord ends
- ☐ 2 4mm silver jump rings
- ☐ 2 10mm decorative silver hoops
- ☐ large silver lobster clasp
- ☐ silver glue-on pendant bail
- ☐ 20-gauge silver wire
- ☐ Six-strand cotton embroidery floss (light green, teal)
- ☐ 4" square of cardboard
- ☐ bead tray (optional)
- ☐ white polymer clay
- ☐ large floral or other print stamp
- ☐ Tim Holtz® Adirondack® Alcohol Ink (Aqua and Sunshine Yellow)
- ☐ Ranger® Mini Ink Blending Tool and Sponge Applicators
- ☐ Ranger® Blending Solution
- ☐ Vintaj® Patina For All Metals (Nouveau Silver)
- ☐ E6000® Industrial Strength Adhesive
- ☐ small paintbrush
- ☐ craft knife
- ☐ deck of playing cards
- ☐ disposable gloves
- ☐ rolling pin and small baking sheet (dedicated to working with clay; do not use with food)
- ☐ wax paper
- ☐ chain-nose pliers (2 pair)
- ☐ round-nose pliers
- ☐ wire cutters

Continued on page 26.

*Be sure to read the **General Instructions** on pages 30-32 before making your project.*

***Necklace Finished Length:** about 28", excluding pendant*

To make the Necklace:

1. To make the pendant, pinch off about half of the clay. Knead and roll the clay in your hand to soften and condition it; roll it into a ball. Lay out two stacks of 18 playing cards each, about 3" apart, on a wax paper covered work surface. Slightly flatten the ball and place it between the card stacks. Using the rolling pin to roll out the clay to the height of the card stacks.

2. Lay the clay shape on the floral stamp and gently roll with the rolling pin to create the design in the clay. Carefully cut a 1" x 2" rectangle with the craft knife. Using your fingers, smooth the sides to give the clay a more rounded shape.

3. To create the hole for the wire loop of the tassel, cut a 2" wire length. Insert the wire about 1/2" into the clay at the center bottom, halfway up the height of the clay shape ***(Photo 1)***. Follow the manufacturer's instructions to bake the clay shape. Once the clay shape has cooled, gently remove the wire and set aside for now.

Photo 1

4. Put on disposable gloves. Place 3-4 drops of Sunshine Yellow ink on the sponge applicator and dab over the entire pendant front. Remove the pad and set aside; attach a new pad to the applicator. Add 3-4 drops of Aqua ink along with a few drops of blending solution. Dab the Aqua ink on the lower section of the pendant, stopping about halfway up. Add a few dabs to the yellow inked section of the pendant. Apply a few more layers of both colors to deepen the colors (changing the applicator between colors), gently "scrubbing" the pad in a circular motion to get color into the recessed areas of the pendant. Apply ink to the pendant back in the same manner. Paint the pendant sides Nouveau Silver.

5. To make the tassel, start at the bottom of the cardboard piece and wrap the teal embroidery floss around the cardboard about 16 times. Trim the floss from the skein. Wrap the light green floss around the cardboard about 7 times; trim the floss from the skein. Slip a 5" strand of light green floss under the floss strands near the top. Knot the floss, trim the ends, and apply a dab of adhesive to the knot. Once dry, hide the knot inside the tassel.

6. Cut the floss along the bottom edge and remove the cardboard. Placing the knot at the back, securely tie a 5" strand of light green floss around the tassel about 1/4" below the folded top edge. Trim the ends and apply a dab of glue to the knot.

7. To complete the pendant, make a wrapped loop with the 2" wire length, slipping the tassel on the loop before wrapping it. Thread the 8mm clear bead on the wire end. Dip the wire end into adhesive and insert the wire into the hole on the bottom of the pendant; allow to dry. Adhere the bail to the top back of the pendant. Allow to dry.

8. Cut a 56" linen cord length. Thread one cord end through one hoop; slide the hoop about 4" onto the cord. Tie 2-3 overhand knots around the longer cord end. Squeeze the knots to "press" them into the wax cord to reduce the bulk. Trim the tail close to the last knot.

9. Using a bead tray or a towel-lined baking sheet, place the pendant at the center front. Starting next to the pendant, lay the beads in the following order for ***each*** side of necklace:
   - lime rondelle bead, 2 aqua rodelle beads, rhinestone rondelle bead, 10mm teal round bead
   - lime rondelle bead, 2 aqua rodelle beads, 10mm clear bead, 2 aqua rondelle beads, lime rondelle bead
   - 10mm teal bead, rhinestone rondelle bead, 2 aqua rondelle beads, lime rondelle bead, 2 aqua rondelle beads, rhinestone rondelle bead, 10mm teal bead
   - lime rondelle bead, 2 aqua rodelle beads, 10mm clear bead, 2 aqua rondelle beads, lime rondelle bead
   - 10mm teal bead, rhinestone rondelle bead, 2 aqua rondelle beads, lime rondelle bead

10. Cut the end of the cord at an angle and twist it tightly to make a "needle" for threading; retrim and twist as needed.

11. Thread the first 5 beads onto the cord, sliding them tight against the knot. Tie an overhand knot, tight against the last bead (use a straight pin to tighten the knot). Thread the next 7 beads onto the cord and tie a knot.Thread the next 9 beads onto the cord and tie a knot. Thread the next 7 beads onto the cord and tie a knot. Thread the next 5 beads onto the cord. You should be at the center front of the necklace. Thread the pendant onto the cord. Thread the remaining beads onto the cord, knotting them in the reverse order from the sequence above.

12. Thread the cord end through the remaining hoop. Tie 2-3 overhand knots and squeeze the knots to "press" them into the wax cord to reduce the bulk. Trim the ends close to the last knot.

13. Lay one suede end in one fold-over cord end, apply a drop of adhesive, and use the chain-nose pliers to fold the tabs down over the suede ***(FIg. 1)***. Repeat with the remaining cord end on the opposite suede end.

Fig. 1

14. Use a 4mm jump ring to attach the fold-over cord end to one hoop. Use the remaining jump ring to join the opposite cord end to the clasp.

SHOPPING LIST

- ☐ 2 5mm x 8mm wooden aqua rondelle beads
- ☐ 2 3mm x 5mm lime green rondelle beads
- ☐ 2 silver ear wires
- ☐ 18-gauge silver wire
- ☐ white polymer clay
- ☐ large floral or other print stamp
- ☐ Tim Holtz® Adirondack® Alcohol Ink (Aqua and Sunshine Yellow)
- ☐ Ranger® Mini Ink Blending Tool and Sponge Applicators
- ☐ Ranger® Blending Solution
- ☐ Vintaj® Patina For All Metals (Nouveau Silver)
- ☐ small paintbrush
- ☐ craft knife
- ☐ deck of playing cards
- ☐ wooden skewer
- ☐ disposable gloves
- ☐ rolling pin and small baking sheet (dedicated to working with clay; do not use with food)
- ☐ wax paper
- ☐ chain-nose pliers (2 pair)
- ☐ round-nose pliers
- ☐ wire cutters

STAMPED EARRINGS

*Be sure to read the **General Instructions** on pages 30-32 before making your project.*

To make each Earring:

1. Follow Steps 1 and 2 of the Stamped Necklace to roll out and stamp the clay. Cut a $^1/_2$" x $1^1/_2$" rectangle of stamped clay. Use the skewer to make a hole at the top of the rectangle. Follow the manufacturer's instructions to bake the clay earring.

2. Once the earring has cooled, follow Step 4 to color the clay earring.

3. Cut a 3" wire length. Make a wrapped loop with the wire, threading the clay earring onto the wire before completing the loop. Thread an aqua rondelle bead and a green rondelle bead on the wire. Make a wrapped loop, attaching the wire to an ear wire.

COLOR OPTION

Create a tropical sunset necklace and earring set for a hot summer night look just by changing the ink colors and beads. Substitute Raspberry ink for the Aqua ink on the pendant and earrings; choose salmon and light orange embroidery floss for the pendant tassel. Choose pale peach seed beads (about 92), 4mm silver ball beads (20), 6mm orange faceted beads (6), and 8mm x 10mm dark peach barrel beads (4). Instead of threading the beads onto a waxed cord for the necklace, thread them onto a 23" length of bead stringing wire, attaching a 4mm silver jump ring at each end. An 8" length of pale peach suede lacing with attached fold-over cord ends completes the necklace. Add pale peach seed beads, orange faceted beads, and the clay pieces to ear wires to make the earrings.

GENERAL INSTRUCTIONS

TOOLS

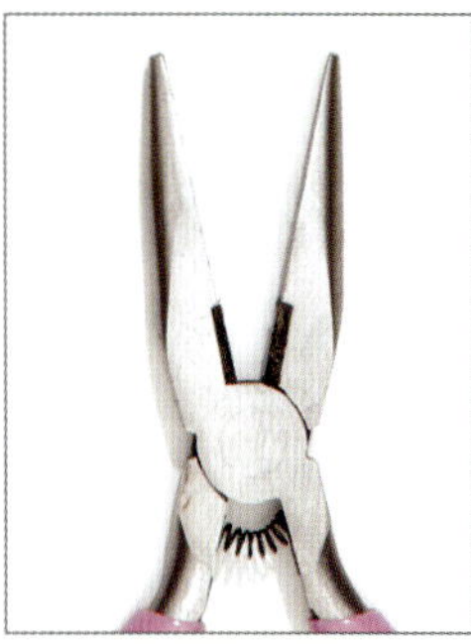

Chain-nose pliers have rounded, tapered jaws and a flat interior surface that will not mar wire. These pliers are used for reaching into tight places, gripping objects, opening and closing jump rings, and bending wire.

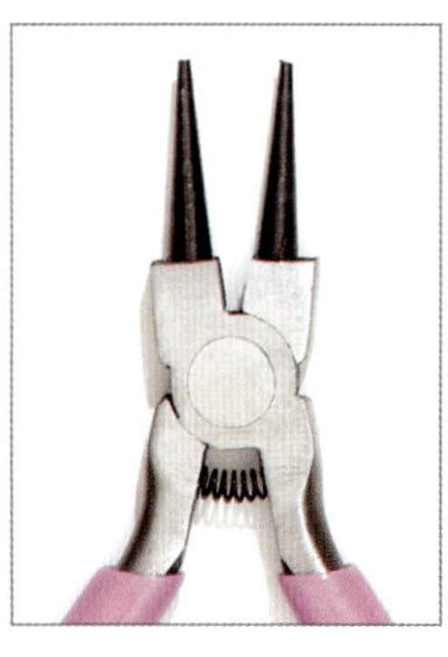

Round-nose pliers have round jaws that are useful for making loops and bending wire smoothly.

Wire cutters are used to cut small gauge wire, head pins, and eye pins.

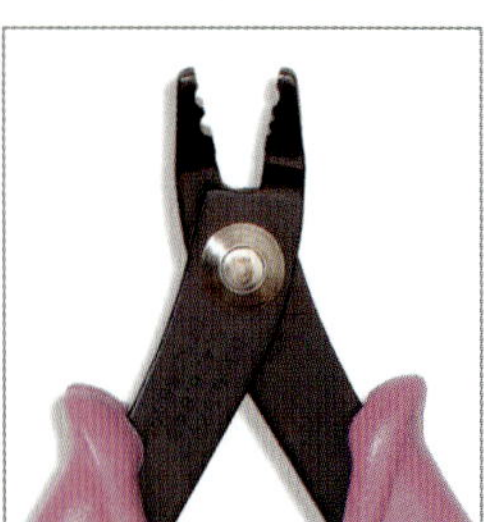

A **crimp tool** (also known as crimping pliers) flattens and shapes the crimp bead or crimp tube.

TECHNIQUES

Opening and Closing Loops, Chain Links, or Jump Rings
Hold one side of the loop, link, or jump ring with chain-nose pliers. With a second pair of chain-nose pliers, gently hold the other side of the loop. Open the loop by pulling one pair of pliers toward you while pushing the other away ***(Fig. 1)***.

Fig. 1

Close the loop by pushing and pulling the pliers in opposite directions, bringing the loop ends back together.

Tying Knots Between Beads
As you tie the overhand knot, slip a straight pin in the knot loop ***(Fig. 2)*** and guide the knot as close to the bead as possible ***(Fig. 3)*** near one end.

Fig. 2

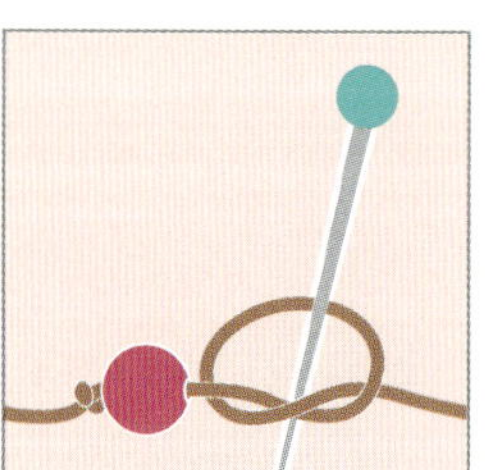

Fig. 3

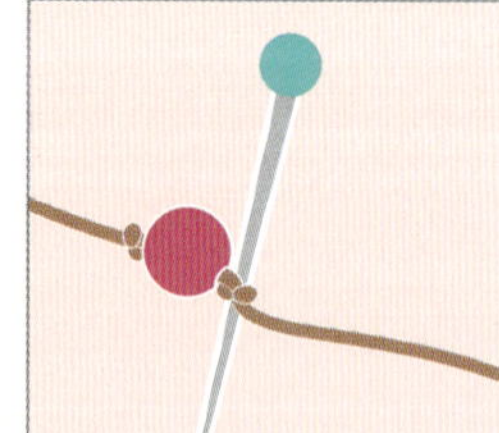

Making Bead Dangles and Bead Connectors

To make a bead dangle, slide the bead(s) on a head pin. Leaving about 1/2", cut off the excess wire. Using chain-nose pliers, bend the wire at a 90° angle ***(Fig. 4)***. Grasp the wire end with the round-nose pliers. Turn the pliers and bend the wire into a loop ***(Figs. 5-6)***. Release the pliers. Straighten or twist the loop further if necessary.

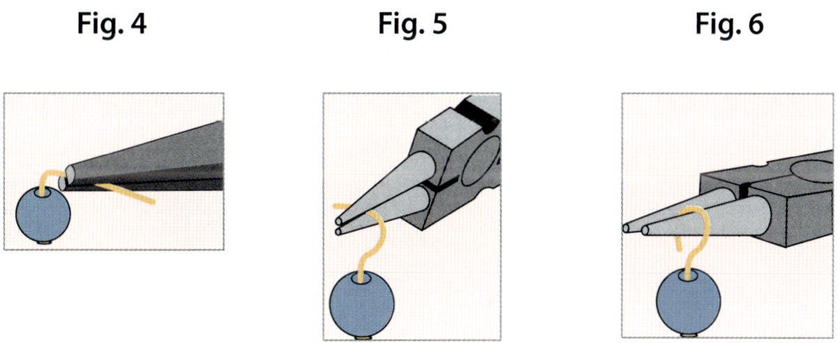

To make a bead connector, slide the bead(s) on an eye pin. Follow bead dangle instructions, above, to make a loop on the end of the eye pin.

Making a Wrapped Loop on a Head Pin, Eye Pin, or Wire End

Slide the bead(s) on a head pin, eye pin, or wire end. Using chain-nose pliers, bend the wire at a 90° angle about 1/8" above the bead ***(Fig. 7)***. Grasp the wire with the round-nose pliers at the 90° bend. Use your finger to push the wire around the barrel of the pliers ***(Fig. 8)***. Remove the pliers. Now is the time to slide the loop onto your project or to add something to the wrapped loop. Holding the loop with the chain-nose pliers, use a second pair of chain-nose pliers to wrap the wire end around itself above the bead 3-5 times ***(Fig. 9)***. Trim the excess wire and tuck the wire end into the wraps with chain-nose pliers.

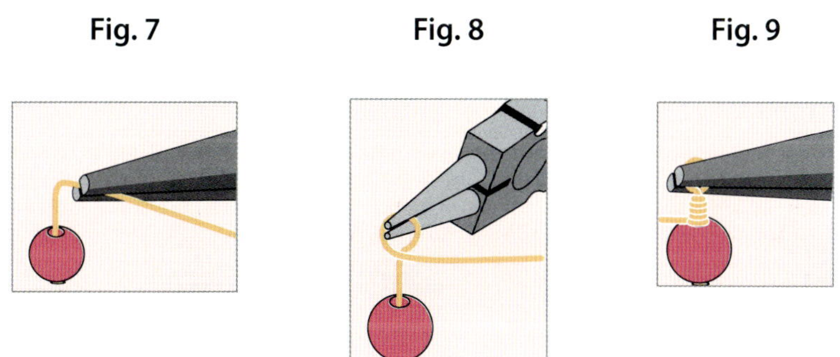

Using Crimp Beads

To finish a wire end, thread a crimp bead and the clasp or jump ring on the wire. Run the wire back through the crimp bead; use a pair of pliers to pull and tighten the wire ***(Fig. 10)***. Place the crimp bead on the inner groove of the crimp tool and squeeze ***(Fig. 11)***.

Release the tool, turn the crimp bead a quarter turn, and place it in the outer groove ***(Fig. 12)***. Squeeze the tool to round out the crimp bead ***(Fig. 13)***. Trim the wire end or if the design calls for beads, thread the beads over the wire to cover the end.

Fig. 10

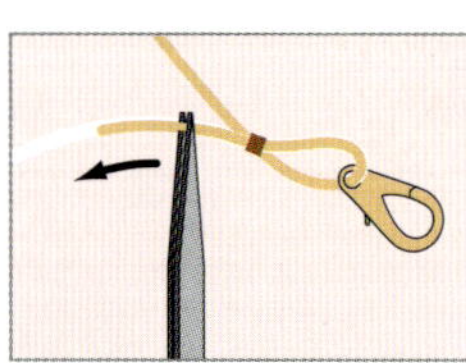

Fig. 11

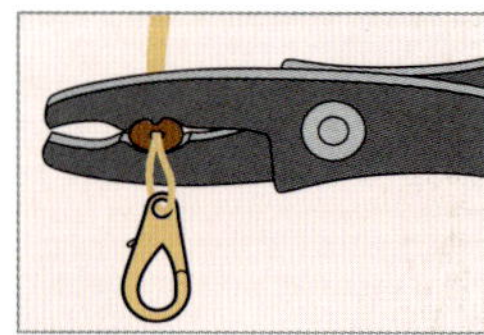

Fig. 12

Fig. 13

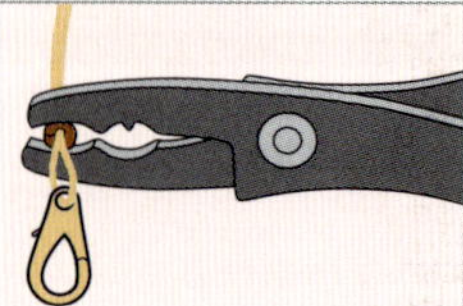

Production Team: Technical Writer – Mary Sullivan Hutcheson; Technical Associate – Lisa Lancaster; Editorial Writer – Susan Frantz Wiles; Senior Graphic Artist – Lora Puls; Graphic Artist – Victoria Temple; Photostylists – Angela Alexander and Sondra Daniel ; Photographers – Jason Masters and Ken West.